ABOVE: **POSEIDON** (Neptune), god of the sea, emerging from
the waves in his shell and dolphin-encrusted chariot drawn
by hippocamps and surrounded by tritons and nereids. He
holds his symbol of power, the trident. From Giovanni Battista
Ferrari's Flora seu de Florum Cultura, Amsterdam, 1646.

First published 2023
This edition © Wooden Books Ltd 2023

Published by Wooden Books Ltd.
Glastonbury, Somerset
www.woodenbooks.com

British Library Cataloguing in Publication Data
Lewis, P.
Pantheon

A CIP catalogue record for this book
may be obtained from the British Library

ISBN-10: 1-907155-49-x
ISBN-13: 978-1-907155-49-9

Designed and typeset in Glastonbury, UK.

Printed in China on FSC® certified papers by
RR Donnelley Asia Printing Solutions Ltd.

PANTHEON

GODS AND GODDESSES
OF THE GRECO-ROMAN WORLD

Philippa Lewis

Thank you to Paul Taylor and the Iconographic Database at the Warburg Institute, London for supplying many of the pictures in this book. Other images have come from rare books in the London Library, and from Wikimedia Commons, the British Museum, the Wellcome Institute, Rijksmuseum, and the Metropolitan Museum of Art.

ABOVE: Detail from the great frieze of the Pergamon altar, c. 170BC, representing the fight of the gods with the Titans and giants. Spearheaded by ZEUS, the Olympian Gods fought the Titans for domination over the universe, a struggle known as the Titanomachy. After their victory, Zeus and his brothers HADES and POSEIDON drew lots for the division of the cosmos; Hades got the underworld, Poseidon the sea and Zeus the heavens and earth. All powerful, he ruled from Mount Olympus.

TITLE PAGE: Zeus among the Olympic Gods.

ABOVE: Hellenistic Marble relief, c.50BC, Taranto, Italy (Walters Art Museum). Left to right: HESTIA (goddess of the hearth), with scepter; HERMES (messenger of the gods), with cap & staff; APHRODITE (goddess of love and beauty), with veil; ARES (god of war), with helmet & spear; DEMETER (goddess of agriculture), with scepter & wheat sheaf; HEPHAESTUS (god of the forge), with staff; HERA (queen of the gods), with scepter; POSEIDON (god of the sea), with trident; ATHENA (goddess of wisdom & the arts), with owl and helmet; ZEUS (king of the gods), with thunderbolt & staff; ARTEMIS (goddess of the hunt & moon), with bow & quiver; and APOLLO (god of the sun), with "kithara." BELOW: The marriage of EROS and PSYCHE, blessed by Zeus. Psyche is one a small number of mortals elevated to deity. Others include GLAUCUS (p.15, who ate a magical herb and became a sea god), Ganymede (p.11) and Britomartis (p.25).

INTRODUCTION

O N MOUNT OLYMPUS, so high its snowy peaks penetrated the heavens, once lived the immortal gods and goddesses of the classical pantheon under the supreme power of Zeus. Originating in Ancient Greece, and largely adopted by the Romans (in this book the Roman names, where they exist, are given in bracketed italics, after the Greek name), these powerful characters and their enfolding mythologies were later absorbed into the artistic and decorative canon of the western world. Their actions and personalities gave them attributes and traits that have provided an iconic short-hand right up to today.

Why else would we find the caduceus of Hermes (*Mercury*) on a post office, the thunderbolt of Zeus (*Jupiter*) over the entrance to a subway station, the vine-wreathed thyrsus of Dionysus (*Bacchus*) on a dining room chimney piece, Apollo's lyre in theatres and concert halls, Athena's helmeted head crowning the portals of libraries, or Poseidon's trident, dolphins and hippocamps on salt cellars and naval dockyards?

Familiarity with the classical pantheon is no longer part of everyone's education, so this book serves as a guide to these gods and goddesses for the modern reader, and to deified mortals, such as Asclepius (*Aesculapius*) or Herakles (*Hercules*), who have frequently stepped in to elucidate and ornament the meaning and purpose of a hospital or nutcracker.

Pantheon means "many gods". The word was also used for a 27BC Roman temple dedicated to all the gods, a 1698 treatise on the gods, a 1772 London entertainment venue and a 1791 Parisian mausoleum for its illustrious dead. The gods live on today, for example, as the names of space programmes, Apollo (20th C.) and Artemis (21st C.).

THE PRIMORDIAL GODS
the first generation

The earliest writings relating to ancient Greek cosmogony (the creation of the universe) and theogony (the birth of the gods) come from the Greek poets Hesiod and Homer, c.700 BC, but these probably record much older oral traditions. The stories begin with primordial elements.

In the beginning was the void, CHAOS (*below*), a dark unbounded space, out of which issued GAIA (or GAEA, later GE, Roman *Tellus*), the personification of Mother Earth, and beneath her an abyss, TARTARUS, where the gods banished their enemies (the opposite of the Elysian Fields, home to the souls of the Blessed).

EROS (god of love and world force), emerged at this time (with a different heritage to the later Eros, *see p.43*), as did EREBUS (*Scotus*, god of shadow and darkness), NYX (*Nox*, goddess of night, *shown right*) and AEON (*Aeternitas*, god of everlasting time).

2

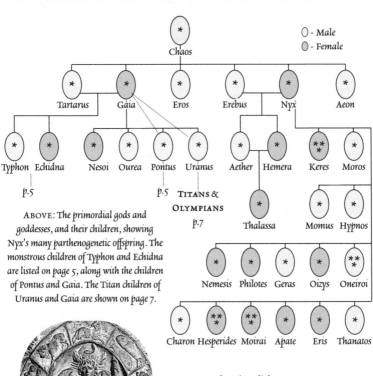

○ - Male
◐ - Female

Chaos

Tartarus — Gaia — Eros — Erebus — Nyx — Aeon

Typhon Echidna   Nesoi Ourea Pontus Uranus   Aether — Hemera   Keres Moros

p.5   p.5 **TITANS &**
                                            OLYMPIANS
                                            p.7

Thalassa   Momus Hypnos

Nemesis Philotes Geras Oizys Oneiroi

Charon Hesperides Moirai Apate Eris Thanatos

ABOVE: The primordial gods and goddesses, and their children, showing Nyx's many parthenogenetic offspring. The monstrous children of Typhon and Echidna are listed on page 5, along with the children of Pontus and Gaia. The Titan children of Uranus and Gaia are shown on page 7.

LEFT: The primordial **EROS-AEON/PHANES** hatched from the world egg, surrounded by the zodiac. Greco-Roman bas relief, c.150AD. FACING PAGE: LEFT: **CHAOS**, the original void. RIGHT: **NYX**, goddess of night. There are other versions of the creation story. E.g. in the Orphic Theogonies **HYDROS** (Water), **THESIS** (Creation) and Mud were the first entities to emerge at the dawn of creation. Mud then solidified into **GAIA** (Earth) who, together with Hydros, produced **KRONOS** (Time) and **ANANKE** (Necessity, Compulsion) who both then produced **PHANES** (Life).

3

THE PRIMORDIAL CHILDREN
the second generation

Of the primordial beings, all but Eros had issue. Hesiod states that from Chaos, Gaia gave birth to URANUS (*Caelus*, god of the starry heavens), PONTUS (god of the sea, father of sea creatures), the OUREA (gods of mountains) and NESOI (goddesses of valleys and islands). By Tartarus, Gaia had the monsters TYPHON (*opposite*) and ECHIDNA. Erebus and Nyx produced AETHER (god of light, spark of life) and HEMERA (*Dies*, god of day), who produced THALASSA (*Mare*, goddess of the sea).

Meanwhile, from Nyx alone came a legion of complications: MOROS (*Fatum*, doom); the KERES (*Letum*, violent death, *p.56*); THANATOS (*Mors*, peaceful death, *p.56*); HYPNOS (*Somnus*, sleep, *p.39*); MOMUS (*Querella*, blame); OIZYS (*Miseria*, pain and distress); PONOS (*Labor*, toil); the HESPERIDES (daughters of night, *p.48*); the MOIRAI (*Parcae*, fates, *p.52*); NEMESIS (*Invidia*, indignation and retribution, *page 57*); APATE (*Fraus*, deceit); PHILOTES (*Amicitia*, friendship); GERAS (*Senectus*, old age); and ERIS (*Discordia*, strife and discord, *opposite lower right & p.18*).

4

LEFT: TYPHON, *son of* GAIA *and* TARTARUS, *a giant, made of fire and serpents. He and his snake partner* ECHIDNA *produced the two-headed dog* ORTHRUS, *the three headed dog* CERBERUS (p.35), *the many-headed* HYDRA, *the fire-breathing* CHIMERA, *the sphinx, the dragon* LADON, *the* COLCHIAN DRAGON, *the monster* SCYLLA (p.14), *and the winged* HARPIES (shown).

FACING PAGE: THALASSA, *goddess of the sea and consort of Pontus.* ABOVE: LEFT: PONTUS, *god the sea. His mother Gaia and he gave birth to sea deities* NEREUS (*calm sea*); THAUMAS (*might of the sea, and father of both* IRIS *the rainbow and the* HARPIES, *storm winds*); EURYBIA; *and finally brother and sister* PHORCYS *and* CETO *who begot the* GRAEAE, (*three fearsome old women who shared one eye and one tooth between them*) *and the three* GORGONS, *the only mortal one,* MEDUSA, *being later slain by the hero* PERSEUS, *her blood in the sea giving rise to* PEGASUS. RIGHT: ERIS, *one of the many children of Nyx.*

5

GAIA & URANUS
the birth of the gods

According to Hesiod, Gaia "first bore starry Heaven (Uranus), equal to herself, to cover her on every side, and to be an ever-sure abiding-place for the blessed gods". By Uranus, she bore the twelve original TITANS, six male and six female: OCEANUS and TETHYS (parents of the 3000 Oceanid nymphs), HYPERION and THEIA (parents of Helios, Selene, Eos, *p.48*), COEUS and PHOEBE (parents of Leto and Asteria), CRONOS and RHEA (forebearers of the Olympian deities), CRIUS (father by Eurybia of Astraeus, Pallas, and Perses), IAPETUS (father of Atlas, Menoetius, Prometheus, and Epimetheus by the Ocean-nymph Clymene), THEMIS (mother of the Horae, *p.58*, and Morai, *p.52*), and MNEMOSYNE (mother of the Muses by Zeus, *p.44*).

Gaia then gave birth to the three CYCLOPS: BRONTES (thunder), STEROPES (lightening) and ARGES (sheet-lightening) (*p.22*); followed by the giant hundred-handed HECATONCHEIRES (Centimanes): COTTUS (earthquake), BRIAREUS (tempestuous sea) and GYES (storm wind).

However, Uranus, fearing that these monsters might seize his power, sealed them in the Earth. Gaia, deeply angered, sought revenge and fashioned a sickle of adamant (diamond), urging her children to punish their father. The youngest, Cronos, then castrated his father with the sickle and assumed control of the cosmos.

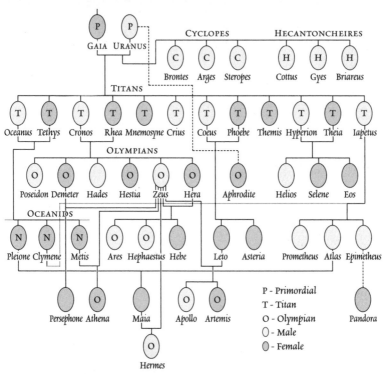

P - Primordial
T - Titan
O - Olympian
◯ - Male
◉ - Female

ABOVE: The Titan children of Gaia and
Uranus, and the Olympian children of Cronos
(Saturn) & Rhea, and the other Olympians.
FACING PAGE: **GAIA** and her children,
including **URANUS** (Heaven), overlooked
by her brother, the primordial **AEON**, shown
standing inside his zodiacal wheel. Greco-
Roman mosaic, c.250AD.
LEFT: Uranus being castrated by his son
CRONOS (Saturn) at Gaia's request. From the
drops of blood were born the **ERINYES** (p.56).

7

CRONOS - SATURN
first among the Titans

CRONOS (*Saturn*) was the youngest of the Titans. He and his sister RHEA (*Ops, Roman goddess of plenty and fertility, top right*) together produced the twelve gods of Olympus. Amongst them were their sons ZEUS (*Jupiter, p.10*), POSEIDON (*Neptune, p.14*), HADES (*Pluto, p.34*), ARES (*Mars, p.18*) and HEPHAESTOS (*Vulcan, p.22*) and daughters HESTIA (*Vesta, p.32*), DEMETER (*Ceres, p.30*) and HERA (*Juno, p.12*).

An oracle predicted that Cronos would be destroyed by his own son, so he devoured his first five children at their birth. However, when Zeus was born, Rhea gave Cronos a stone swaddled like a baby (*opposite, top left*) which he ate instead. He later vomited up all these swallowed children, and Zeus then led his brothers and sisters in a war against the Titans (*see below, and frontispiece*), eventually imprisoning his father Cronos in a cavity beneath Tartarus.

Cronos stands for the forces of nature, both good and bad, for fertility and floods. His expression is saturnine. He is depicted as Father Time (*Chronos* means 'time' in Greek): an old semi-naked figure with scythe, winged hourglass and crutch, he waves a snake with its tail in its mouth, symbol of eternity. As a symbol of time passing, he appears on clocks, weathervanes, *chronometers*, gravestones and memorials.

8

ABOVE: LEFT: Rhea hands Cronos a stone, instead of Zeus. RIGHT: The immortal Centaur **CHIRON**, offspring of Cronos and the Oceanid **PHILYRA** (to escape censure from Rhea Cronos transformed into a stallion, hence Chiron's form, half man, half horse).

ABOVE: **CRONOS** (Saturn) armed with the sickle given to him by his mother Gaia, used to castrate his father Uranus. He rides in a chariot drawn by dragons. The Roman god Saturn, (whose December festival Saturnalia prefigured Christmas) was a god of agriculture and also carried a scythe, and so became identified with Cronos.

9

ZEUS - JUPITER
ruler of Olympus

ZEUS (*Jupiter* to the Romans) was the supreme God of the classical pantheon. With his first wife METIS (*Prudence*) he fathered ATHENA (*Minerva, p.16*). With his second wife THEMIS (*Justice*) he had the HORAE (*p.58*), ASTRAEA (*p.54*) and MOIRAE (*p.52*). His third wife and queen was HERA (*p.12*), mother of HEPHAESTUS (*Vulcan, p.22*), ARES (*Mars, p.18*) and HEBE (*Juventas, p.12*). He tangled with many goddesses, producing PERSEPHONE (*Proserpina, p.30 & 34*) with DEMETER (*Ceres, p.30*), APOLLO (*p.26*) and ARTEMIS (*Diana, p.24*) with LETO, APHRODITE (*Venus*) with DIONE, the MUSES (*p.44*) with MNEMOSYNE, BACCHUS (*Dionysus, p.36*) with SEMELE, the GRACES (*p.21*) with EURYNOME, HERMES (*Mercury, p.28*) with MAIA and HERAKLES (*Hercules, p.40*) with ALKEMENE. The Greek poet Hesiod [c.750–650 BC] called him '*cloud-gatherer; high-seated; loud-thundering; counselling; mild; wide-seeing*'.

Omniscient ruler of heaven and earth and demanding obedience from gods and men, Zeus, majestic, bearded, grandiosely enthroned, maintains law and order, with the help of THEMIS (*p.54*), NEMESIS (*p.56*) and DIKE (*p.54*). His sceptre of cypress symbolises eternity and power. Both good and evil originate from him, and according to whim he assigns fates to kings and beggars alike.

The Romans named the largest planet in the solar system after him: *Jupiter*.

ZEUS was the master of metamorphosis. FACING PAGE: As a swan, he seduced the mortal LEDA; who then produced two eggs, one hatching the DIOSCURI, twins CASTOR and POLLUX, the other, HELENA (Helen of Troy), the most beautiful woman in Greece. LEFT: In the guise of an eagle Zeus seized the beautiful Trojan youth GANYMEDE (Catamitus) and transported him to Mount Olympus where he was granted immortality and, on Hebe's marriage to Herakles, he succeeded her as cup-bearer to the Gods. To DANAE (who then gave birth to Perseus) he appeared as a shower of gold; to ANTIOPE a satyr; to EUROPA a bull; to the nymph CLYTORIS as an ant, and to ALCEMENA, mother of Herakles (p.40) he came as her husband, Amphytrion.

ABOVE: ZEUS, riding his eagle, symbol for ambitious rulers of all ages. He clutches thunder and lightning bolts, forged for him by Hephaestus and the Cyclops, with which he killed Typhon (p.5), Aesklepius (p.38) and Phaeton (p.48). Zeus' bolts have long been used to imply fire and power, as on arsenals and electrical facilities (e.g. Bank Underground entrance in London).

HERA – JUNO
goddess of marriage and childbirth

HERA (*Juno*) was daughter of CRONOS (*Saturn, p.8*) and RHEA, and sister and wife of ZEUS (*Jupiter, p.10*). By him she gave birth to ARES (*Mars, p.18*), HEPHAESTUS (*Vulcan, p.22*) and HEBE (*Juventus, shown opposite*), the wife of Herakles, who waited on the gods, filling their cups with rejuvenating nectar. Hera was the goddess of marriage. At her unorthodox wedding (the only true marriage among the Olympian deities) a tree bore golden apples and streams of ambrosia sprang from the ground. She was famously vindictive (unsurprising given Zeus's multiple infidelities) and the couples' battles were violent (Zeus once hung her on chains from the clouds with anvils suspended from her feet), often felt on earth as sudden storms. She persecuted HERMES (*Mercury, p.28*) and HERAKLES (*p.40*), Zeus' children by mortal mothers.

The figure of Hera is dignified and junoesque (*right*). She wears a royal diadem from which a star-spangled veil falls down her back. She is enthroned Queen of Heaven, a position matched by her ego and vanity. The peacock, as symbol for air, is sacred to her, its 100 tailfeather 'eyes' those of ARGOS, the giant killed by Hermes. She protected women during childbirth, holding a pomegranate, symbol of fertility.

ABOVE: **HERA** (Juno) seated between her husband **ZEUS** (Jupiter) and their daughter **HEBE** (Juventus), cupbearer to the gods, beside **IRIS** (Arcus), messenger to the gods and goddess of the rainbow. Hera was associated with peacocks, cuckoos (Zeus seduced her as one), lilies and cows.

LEFT: **EILEITHIA** (Lucina), light-bringer, was another daughter of Hera and Zeus. She was goddess of childbirth and labour pains. The picture shows the beautiful youth **ADONIS** (see too page 20) being born from his mother **SMYRNA** (who the gods in pity had transformed into a myrrh tree) and delivered into the arms of kind Lucina.

13

POSEIDON – NEPTUNE
god of the sea

After the war with the Titans, Zeus and his two brothers drew lots for supremacy. POSEIDON (*Neptune*) came second, and chose power over the sea and all waters. His wife was the nereid AMPHITRITE, with whom he fathered the merman TRITON. He fathered scores more children with more than forty other goddesses, nymphs and humans, including the sea-monster CHARYBDIS with Gaia, the winged horse PEGASUS with Medusa, and the hero THESEUS with Aethra.

He had extraordinary physical strength (Homer called him the Earth-convulser). He is shown bearded and splendid, armed with a trident, cracking rocks and beating the land to bring rain, dew and springs to fill streams and rivers to feed the seas and oceans. By generating earthquakes he created mountains and islands. By his mastery over water he formed rain clouds to water crops and livestock. Sea-monsters and floods were his weapons, and winds were under his command.

He is seen with TRITONS (half fish/man mermen), NEREIDS (sea-nymphs), seaweed, shells, dolphins and other marine creatures. His ornamentation appears on all things watery: fountains, ships' figure-heads, salt-cellars, water jugs, bathrooms and naval buildings.

ABOVE: LEFT: *The merman* TRITON, *Poseidon & Amphitrite's son, controlled the waves by blowing on a conch shell.* RIGHT: *Triton consorting with one of the* NEREIDS.

ABOVE: POSEIDON, *speeding across the waves on a shell-chariot pulled by* HIPPOCAMPS, *with his wife* AMPHITRITE *(Salacia), goddess of salt water, often shown robed with nets and lobster claws in her hair. Together they inhabited a dazzling undersea palace.*
FACING PAGE, LEFT / CENTRE: *The parents of Amphitrite and the other 49* NEREIDES *(sea nymphs) were the Oceanid* DORIS *and* NEREUS *"The Old Man of the Sea".* RIGHT: *The sea fisherman god* GLAUCUS *courting* SCYLLA, *later turned into a sea monster by Circe.*

ATHENA – MINERVA
goddess of wisdom

The goddess **ATHENA** (*Minerva*), was born from Zeus' head in the midst of a black tempest cloud. Zeus had earlier swallowed her pregnant mother, the Oceanid nymph Metis, after having been warned that a son would destroy him. Athena inherited martial power from her father and wisdom from her mother, a powerful combination that made her one of the most revered and useful of goddesses. In her role as warrior, she was **PALLAS ATHENA**, goddess of victorious battles, protector of the state and defender of virtue against enemies.

Victory leads to peace, and peace to prosperity. Thus, Athena also governs education, civilising handicrafts such as spinning and weaving, and agriculture. She devised the plough and rake, and planted the first olive tree (a winning move in her contest with Poseidon to gain patronage of Athens).

She is symbolised by two birds: the owl, that can see in the dark, clear-sighted when others are blind, and the cockerel, a fighting bird. As a civic heroine who is also goddess of wisdom, she became a symbol of municipal endeavour and good government, an obvious ornamentation for parliaments, libraries and learned institutions, like an *Athenaeum* (literary or scientific club), or a *Minerval* (a gift given by scholar to master).

ABOVE: Two illustrations from ancient Greek pottery, c.450BC. LEFT: Poseidon (Neptune) looks on as Hephaestus (Vulcan) cleaves Zeus' head, releasing the infant Athena (Minerva) from Zeus' head. RIGHT: Athena holding her crested helmet, with her owl, symbol of wisdom, knowledge, and insight, ward against evil spirits and token of good fortune.

FACING PAGE: Three aspects of Athena: as Warrior (represented by the cockerel at her feet), as Craftswoman (represented by a distaff) and as wise Arboriculturalist, planter of trees.

LEFT: Athena and her attributes. Her shield has the head of MEDUSA, one of the three snake-haired Gorgans. It was Athena's loan of a polished shield to the hero PERSEUS which enabled him to reflect the Gorgan's petrifying gaze and behead her. From the blood of Medusa's remains rose the winged horse PEGASUS, that flew Perseus to safety.

17

ARES – MARS
god of war

The son of Zeus and Hera, **ARES** (*Mars*) started out as the god of storm and tempest, but soon evolved into the god of war in all its most terrible aspects. He was often accompanied into battle by his sister **ERIS** (*Discordia, p.5*), goddess of strife and discord and wife **ENYO** (*Bellona*), goddess of war (*opposite lower right*). He was disliked and feared, except by Aphrodite (*Venus*), with whom he fathered **HARMONIA** (*Concordia, shown below*), **ANTERUS** (*god of requited love*), and the twins **PHOBOS** (*fear/ panic*) and **DEIMOS** (*terror*). He disarmed only when making love to her, while **EROS** (*Cupid*) played with his armour. With the vestal virgin **RHEA SILVA**, he fathered **ROMULUS** and **REMUS**.

The red planet was named for Mars, associating it with bloodshed (the redness of rusty iron oxide hematite further connecting Mars and iron). The month of March comes from *Martius*, the first month of the earliest Roman calendar, named after Mars. His ornamentation adorns all things *martial*, powerful and aggressive.

NIKE (*Victoria, right*) is the goddess of victory and appeared as a charioteer when Zeus defeated the Titans. A draped figure she has vast wings, flying over the earth spreading news of victory, be it at games, festivals or in battle. She blows a trumpet to announce the good news, and brings the victor the Olympic insignia of victory, a laurel wreath, palm-frond or trophy.

ABOVE: **ARES** (Mars) is often shown armed with a fierce expression, helmet, breastplate, sword or long spear, and shield, riding a chariot drawn by two horses or by his sacred wolves of rapaciousness and perspicacity (who famously suckled his sons Romulus & Remus). His bird is a woodpecker. Later 16th-18th century images show him with contemporary weapons and cannon. BELOW: LEFT: Ares disarms for Aphrodite, helped by Cupid. RIGHT: **ENYO** (Bellona), goddess of war, wife of **ARES** (Mars), leading the imperial Austrian army into battle.

APHRODITE – VENUS
goddess of love

Stories differ as to the birth of **VENUS**; she was either the daughter of Zeus (*Jupiter, p.10*) and the Oceanid Dione, or was fathered by Uranus when his castrated genitals were thrown in the sea by Cronos (*Saturn, p.8*), from which foam she emerged on a scallop shell. She was unsuccessfully married to Hephaestus (*Vulcan, p.22*). By Hermes (*Mercury, p.28*) she produced **EROS** (*Cupid, p.43*) and by Ares (*Mars*) bore further children (*p.18*). She had other entanglements, including with handsome Adonis.

Venus's role stretched from divine love through to fertility and prostitution. Divinely beautiful, she could imbue people with beauty, invincible charm, mirth and joy. Anyone who wore her magic girdle became an object of love and desire. She holds a flaming torch or heart, symbol of hot passion. She and her frequent companion Eros are armed with bows and arrows to pierce the heart. Swans, doves and swallows are sacred to her, as are roses, myrtle and apples. Dice and mirrors are later attributes.

She is the brightest and most beautiful of the five planets. Water is her element, copper her metal. She appears in words like *venerous*, *venereal* and *aphrodisiac*. Hesiod called her: '*smile-loving; well-garlanded; golden; quick-winking; well-tressed; care-dissolving; artful; of sweet pleasure, intimacy, and tenderness.*'

ABOVE: LEFT: **APHRODITE** (Venus) with her handmaidens, the three **GRACES** (Charites/
Gratiae): **EUPHROSYNE** (mirth), **AGLAIA** (elegance) and **THALIA** (youth and beauty).
RIGHT: *Venus with her spear, flaming heart, and astrological Taurus & Libra.*

ABOVE: **APHRODITE** (Venus), riding with **EROS** (Amor/Cupid). FACING PAGE: *Aphrodite
carried by Tritons, emerging from the sea, born from the foam of Uranus' castrated gonads.*

HEPHAESTUS – VULCAN
god of fire and forge

Born lame and weak, HEPHAESTUS (*Vulcan*) was thrown off Mount Olympus by his disgusted mother Hera. Exiled, he was saved by the nereid nymph Thetis and the oceanid nymph Eurynome, with whom he lived for nine years in a grotto below Oceanus, learning smithing. He was the artist among the gods, and according to Homer created metal automaton servants. On his return to Olympus, in retaliation, he fixed Hera to a magical golden throne, demanding Zeus give him the hand of APHRODITE (*Venus*) in return for her release. Zeus agreed. When Hephaestus later discovered his wife's infidelity with ARES (*Mars*) he forged a net of chains to bind them together for the other gods to mock (*see opposite*). Hephaestus became infatuated with Athena when making weapons for her, but she famously refused his advances.

Hephaestus has forges on Olympus, on volcanic islands and deep within the earth. With the one-eyed Cyclops he made Aphrodite's girdle, Hermes' winged helmet, Zeus's thunderbolt, Poseidon's trident, Artemis' bow and arrows and the first human woman, Pandora (*opposite*).

The Romans also called him MULCIBER, melter of metals. He was the god for all arts using fire: smithing, metalwork and pottery. From him we have *volcanologists*, *volcanoes* and *vulcanized vulcanite* (rubber treated with immense heat). Even today, his figure towers over steel-making Sheffield from the top of the Victorian Town Hall clock tower.

ABOVE: **HEPHAESTUS** (Vulcan) at his anvil making weapons, aided by the **CYCLOPS**.

ABOVE: Hephaestus finds his wife Aphrodite in bed with Ares and captures them in a net.

FACING PAGE: Zeus punished the Titan **PROMETHEUS**, who had stolen the fire of the gods for humanity, by chaining him to a rock where his liver was pecked out by eagles every day. To punish mankind he ordered Hephaestus to fashion womankind, **PANDORA**, out of clay.

LEFT: **EPIMETHEUS**, Prometheus' twin, opens Pandora's jar, releasing miseries, sicknesses and other ills into the world.

ARTEMIS - DIANA
moon goddess of the hunt

Twin sister of **APOLLO** (*Phoebus. p.26*), **ARTEMIS** (*Diana*) is the eternally young virgin goddess of wild spaces, wild animals and hunting. She was the daughter of **ZEUS** (*Jupiter, p.10*) and **LETO** (*Latona*). Hera was so jealous of them that she ordered that no-one should shelter Leto while she gave birth, and then sent Python to kill her and the twins (*below right*). Like Pan, she belonged to Arcadia, with its mountains and wooded fertile valleys. With her virgin nymphs and dryads she hunted game and mortals. She caught the giant hunter Orion, and after Actaeon watched her bathe naked she turned him into a stag, to be killed by his own hunting dogs (*see opposite*). She stopped the winds in the Trojan War, stranding King Agamemnon's fleet after he killed her sacred deer.

As Apollo brings day so Artemis became associated with the Moon, bringing nightfall, a crescent moon shining in her hair, representing modesty, chastity and good upbringing.

She was later identified with the moon goddesses **SELENE** (*Luna, p.48*) and **HECATE** (*Trivia, p.34*). Her attributes suit the decoration of hunting lodges (*below*), stables and sporting guns. Silver is her metal. Her temple at Ephesus was one of the seven wonders of the world.

ABOVE: **ARTEMIS** (Diana) was taller and stronger than any other goddess. She often is shown wearing a short tunic for speedy movement, sometimes with an animal skin across her shoulders, holding a bow and a quiver of arrows.

LEFT: The Cretan nymph **BRITOMARTIS** (Dictynna, "daughter of the nets"), child of **ZEUS**, companion of Artemis, was pursued for nine months by King **MINOS** until she leapt into the sea, was saved by a fisherman's net, and was changed into a goddess by Artemis.

APOLLO - PHOEBUS
god of light and music

God of music, **APOLLO** (*Phoebus*) was the son of Zeus and Leto (*p.10*), and twin brother of **ARTEMIS** (*Diana, p.24*). He fathered **ASCLEPIUS** (*Aesculapius, p.38*) with the mortal Coronis, **ARISTAEUS** by the nymph **CYRENE**, possibly **ORPHEUS** with the Muse **CALLOPE** (*p.44*), and numerous demi-gods and mortals.

Like the sun god Helios (*p.48*), Apollo rides a solar chariot across the heavens each morning; his head emanates sun rays, providing a favourite ornament for sources of light and warmth, e.g. candelabra and chimney pieces. When Louis XIV chose the sun as his emblem (Le Roi Soleil) the Apolline head had popular currency at Versailles.

The laurel wreath on Apollo's head derives from his love for the nymph **DAPHNE** who escaped him by turning into a laurel tree. Such wreaths were worn by victors, poets and writers. Holding his lyre, he presides over the Muses (*p.44*), with whom he provides an obvious symbol for theatres and concert halls.

Apollo also protects flocks and herds and is the god of prophecy and divination. Significant animals surrounding him include: cocks (fortell the sunrise); grasshoppers (need heat to sing); swans (have powers of divination); hawks (eyes as bright as the sun); crows (foretell the weather) and wolf (the shepherd's enemy).

ABOVE: LEFT: **APOLLO** (Phoebus) *slaying* **PYTHON**, *the serpent of Delphi, overlooked by the nine muses. He is often depicted as the ideal of young male beauty.* RIGHT: *Apollo being introduced to Music by Athena, patroness of the Arts. He holds his lyre, which had been fashioned by Hermes from a tortoise shell (see p.28).*

LEFT: **DAPHNE** is transformed into a laurel tree to escape Apollo's clutches. Apollo, like Artemis, is often shown with bow and arrows.

FACING PAGE: **ARISTAEUS**, the son of **APOLLO** and the huntress river nymph **CYRENE**. He taught men to keep bees, and was god of flocks, shepherds, vines and olives. Gaia, Chiron, the Horai (seasons) and the Muses all had a hand in his education. He was the Father of Actaeon (p.24).

27

HERMES – MERCURY
god of communication

Son of **ZEUS** (*Jupiter, p.10*) and **MAIA** (one of the seven nymphs of the Pleiades), brother to **APHRODITE** (*Venus, p.20*), **HERMES** (*Mercury*) was appointed herald and messenger for the Mount Olympus deities by his father. His caduceus (staff of negotiation), with its winged tip and entwined snakes resembles the Rod of Asclepius. He received it from **APOLLO** (*p.26*) in exchange for a lyre fashioned from a tortoiseshell.

Hermes is the god of eloquence, explanations and interpretations. As inventor of the alphabet he is a perfect symbol for newspapers, telecom companies and post offices. As a messenger, he has been used for branding on petrol, aviation and international flower delivery (*below*). Herms, boundary posts surmounted by his head, were named for him and later appropriated for garden ornaments (*opposite*).

Hermes is the god of gain (both honest and dishonest) so stands for commerce, money, trading weights and measures and good fortune, appearing on offices, shops and exchanges. An inveterate pilferer (he stole oxen from Apollo, tools from **HEPHAESTUS** (*p.22*), a girdle from **APHRODITE** (*p.20*) and a sceptre from Zeus, he is the god of thieves.

BY WIRE – TO ANY PART OF THE WORLD IN A FEW HOURS

The Romans named the smallest and fastest of the planets *Mercury*, and the chemical element (Hg, or quicksilver) *mercury*. From him we have *mercurial*, *hermetic* and *hermeneutics*.

ABOVE: **HERMES** (Mercury). He has a winged hat (petasus), winged sandals (talaria) and herald's caduceus (which allows unmolested passage). LEFT: **HERMES** (Mercury) and the trades he rules over. BELOW: LEFT: A **HERM**, or boundary post (Roman **TERMINUS**). RIGHT: **HERMAPHRODITUS**, the child of Hermes and **APHRODITE**, was born a boy, but fused with the naiad **SALMACIS**.

DEMETER – CERES
goddess of the abundant harvest

Daughter of **CRONOS** and **RHEA** (*Saturn and Ops, p.8*), and sister of **HADES** (*Pluto, p.34*) and **ZEUS** (*Jupiter, p.10*), **DEMETER** (*Ceres*) married a Cretan farmer, **JASION**, with whom she had a son **PLAUTOS** (*Plutus, p.53*), god of wealth. She was goddess of earth, agriculture and husbandry, symbolised by a cornucopia full of produce (the horn having been torn off **ACHELOUS**, a river god disguised as a bull, by Hercules). Her breasts are full of divine milk, which she fed to **TRIPTOLEMUS** before sending him out to spread seed and the art of agriculture (*opposite*).

With her brother Zeus she had a daughter **PERSEPHONE** (*Proserpina*), worshipped as **KORE** (*Core, the maiden*) who was taken to the underworld by Hades for his wife. Demeter's deep despair over the loss of her daughter caused the harvests to fail, so Zeus intervened: Persephone would spend spring to harvest with her mother, and the barren winter months with her husband in the underworld. Zeus gave Demeter a poppy to help her sleep and forget. This agrarian story was the focus of the Eleusinian mysteries, whose secret religious rites "promised mankind passage to a blessed afterlife".

Ceres and her attributes of plenty embellish corn exchanges, agricultural halls, and centres of commerce. She personified Summer and harvest From her we have *cereal*.

ABOVE: LEFT: **DEMETER** (Ceres) is often shown wreathed with wheat ears, carrying a sickle or torch, and a sheaf of corn or cornucopia of produce. RIGHT: Demeter searches the underworld for her daughter **PERSEPHONE** (Prosperina), abducted by **HADES** (Pluto).

LEFT: Demeter bids farewell to the mortal **TRIPTOLEMUS**, inventor of the plough, off to spread seedcorn across the world using her dragon-drawn chariot. He was later deified.

FACING PAGE: Another agricultural deity, the male-female guardian spirit **PALES**, Roman god of herds, herdsmen flocks and shepherds.

HESTIA – VESTA
goddess of the home and hearth

HESTIA (*Vesta*) was daughter of CRONOS and RHEA (*Saturn and Ops, p.8*), and sister of ZEUS (*Jupiter, p.10*), HERA (*Juno, p.12*), POSEIDON (*Neptune, p.14*), HADES (*Pluto, p.34*) and DEMETER (*Ceres, p.30*). She was wooed by both Poseidon and Apollo (*p.26*) but instead vowed perpetual virginity by placing her hand on the head of Zeus, who granted her the special honour of being worshipped in every home.

Hestia was the embodiment of home and family life, her domesticity represented by the benign fire of the hearth. In public buildings her shrine represented the heart of the state itself, a national family. The first mouthful of every meal was consecrated to her, and a mother would take fire from her sacred flame to a new bride's hearth. Her circular temple in Rome contained no statue, only an eternal sacred flame, tended by her chaste vestal virgins. Her sacred animal was an ass. Bakers adopted Hestia as their patron deity with a millstone emblem.

Goddess of of the sanctity of the home, she was seldom depicted until the 19th century (*see opposite*). Other domestic gods are the Roman LARES, tutelary deities of the house, family and ancestors, and the small puppet-like PENATES, kindly domestic gods of the hearth and household, who provided its daily needs (*right*).

Vesta was the name of mid-19th century wax matches, and *vestal* was until recently a term for *virginal* (or chaste).

32

LEFT: **HESTIA** (Vesta). Modestly draped and veiled she usually holds a lamp or sacrificial plate and a ruler's sceptre. BELOW: A 20th century depiction of Hestia, ornamenting the façade of Eltham Palace, Surrey, home in the 1930s to Stephen and Virginia Courtauld, famous for their lavish entertaining.

FACING PAGE: Two Roman agricultural **LARES** (seated) with small **PENATES** (hanging in the trees). BELOW: The Vestal Virgins (or Vestals), priestesses of Vesta, tend the sacred hearth and flame of ancient Rome. Hestia (Vesta) was also goddess of bakers, and the Romans also had **FORNAX**, divine personification of the oven, who ensured an even heat.

HADES – PLUTO
god of the underworld

HADES (*Pluto*), God of the Underworld, was son of CRONOS and RHEA and brother of Zeus and Poseidon. When the three brothers divided the universe, Hades took the netherwold with dominion over the dead. His wife is PERSEPHONE, daughter of his sister DEMETER (*p.30*). The Romans called him Pluto ("rich"), referring to the mineral wealth of the Earth. Roman poets also called him DIS PATER and ORCUS.

The hellish underworld of Hades is dark and threatening, and the god's mien is appropriately grim: over his long and tangled locks he wears a pointed diadem, and he carries a bident, a forked staff. The cyclops made him a helmet which rendered the wearer invisible.

The souls of the buried dead were conveyed into the underworld over the rivers Styx and Acheron by the ferryman CHARON (*opposite*), son of EREBUS and NYX (*p.2*), guided by the triple goddess HECATE (*right*). The 3-headed hound KERBEROS, (*Cerberus*) draped in serpents, guards the entrance. After dying the dead went to the infernal shades and stygian gloom of Erebus in the far west, never penetrated by the light of sun, moon or stars and surrounded by poplars and weeping willows (often an ornament for gravestones).

In the 1930s, a newly discovered dwarf planet, the ninth, was named Pluto.

ABOVE: **ZEUS**, **POSEIDON** and **HADES** divide the world between them. LEFT: *The Underworld, with ferryman* **CHARON**, *and* **HADES** & **PERSEPHONE** *seated in the shadows. Hades carries the key to the gates of death.* BELOW: **ORPHEUS** *and* **EURIDYCE** *almost escape* **CERBERUS**. FACING PAGE: **HECATE** (Trivia), *Titan deity of twilight, crossroads, magic, souls of the dead and sorcery, who protected travel.*

DIONYSUS – BACCHUS
god of wine

DIONYSUS (*Bacchus*) was son of Zeus and the priestess SEMELE, who Zeus had accidentally killed with a thunderbolt, transplanting the fetus into his thigh. When DIONYSUS (*Bacchus*) was born, to protect him from jealous Hera, Zeus turned him into a kid goat and entrusted him to HERMES (*Mercury, p.28*)who in turn entrusted him to nymphs.

He had two sons by APHRODITE (*Venus, p.20*), HYMENAEUS (god of Marriage) and PRIAPOS (phallic god of fruitfulness, *p.47*), and married ARIADNE after she had been abandoned by THESEUS on Naxos.

Dionysus was first to cultivate the vine. God of wine, he rules both the mirth and madness of drinking. He wanders ceaselessly, his chariot pulled by panthers, accompanied by his cupbearer COMUS (god of festive revels and nocturnal dalliances), SILENUS (a jovial bald old man, too drunk to stand, usually astride an ass or wine barrel), PAN (*Faunus, p.42*), and his THIASUS—a vinous retinue of wildly dancing companions including hairy horned satyrs, wild nymphs, frenzied MAENADS (*Bacchantes*) and orgiastic THYIADES (half ecstatic women with dishevelled hair, cymbals, flutes, serpents and thyrsi waving).

Dining rooms, tableware, theatres, pubs, hotels and all other places of *bacchanalian* festivity are ripe for baccchic ornament.

LEFT: Perennially youthful with a sinuous stance, unmuscular body and knowing tipsy smile, **DIONYSUS** (Bacchus) is easily recognisable. Naked, he is often shown crowned with ivy and vine leaves and holding his attributes of a drinking cup and thyrsus, a rod surmounted with a pinecone, entwined with vine tendrils.

BELOW: Dionysus leads a bacchanalian procession. He holds a ribboned thyrsus (pine-cone tipped staff). Behind him follows drunken **SILENUS** on an ass, and **PAN** (Faunus), a music-making satyr and a snake-waving **THYIASOTE**.

FACING PAGE: Dionysus offers Aphrodite his cup, under the vines, while his panther, Hermes and others look on.

ASCLEPIUS – AESCULAPIUS
god of medicine and healing

ASCLEPIUS (*Aesculapius*) was the mortal son of APOLLO and CORONIS, a Thessalian princess. His mother was killed just before giving birth, but Apollo saved the infant and entrusted him to the centaur CHIRON (*p.9*). He married EPIONE by whom he had five daughters, among them HYGIEA, goddess of health, PANACEA, goddess of herbal healing, and three sons including TELESPHORUS, the child god of convalescence.

Asclepius learnt the healing arts from Chiron and became so skilled that he could bring the dead to life, using restorative blood from the right side of a Gorgon, given him by Athena. Pluto, worried about the depopulation of the underworld, complained to Zeus, who killed Asclepius with a thunderbolt. He was deified after his death.

Asclepius and his children oversee all things medical. His knotted rod entwined with a snake is the symbol for medical foundations, hospitals and pharmacies. The knots represent the difficulty of learning medicine; the snake symbolises renewal, as it sheds its skin to reveal a new one.

His daughter Hygiea (cleanliness and *hygiene*) ornaments the Georgian portico to Bath's Pump Room & Roman Baths.

ABOVE: LEFT: **APOLLO** *gives the infant* **ASCLEPIUS** *to the centaur* **CHIRON**. RIGHT: *Asclepius with his knotted staff entwined with a snake, and a cockerel (for vigilance).* FACING PAGE: *Asclepius, with his cloaked and hooded son,* **TELESPHOROS** (*convalescent care*) *and daughter* **HYGEIA** (*cleanliness*), *shown with her bowl entwined with snake.*

ABOVE: LEFT: *Asclepius's daughter* **PANACEA** (*universal remedy*). CENTRE: *Also essential to healing is the god of sleep* **HYPNOS** (*Somnos*), *son of Nyx (p.2), shown with winged head and inverted torch.* RIGHT: *The Oneiroi, the 1000 children of Hypnos and the Karite Pasithea, include* **MORPHEUS** (*Somnia*), *god of dreams, and* **PHOBETOR** (*nightmares*) *and* **PHANTASUS**.

HERAKLES - HERCULES
the deified hero

Son of **ZEUS** (*Jupiter, p.10*) and **ALCEMENE** (wife of the King of Thebes), Herakles was a hero who was eventually deified. Synonymous with strength and bravery, he appears bearded and muscled, the pelt of the Nemean lion (from the first of his twelve labours) draped around his shoulders, paws dangling over his chest, with the lion's mask forming a helmet. He is often depicted with his massive club, though his armoury also includes poisoned arrows and a burning torch.

It was the tragic killing of his first wife Megara and their children—in a fit of madness sent by vindictive Hera—that indirectly resulted in his being set the twelve herculaean tasks (*see opposite*). His third wife was Hera's daughter **HEBE** (*Juventus, p.12*). He fathered innumerable children, including 50 sons by the 50 daughters of King Thespius.

Herakles' height was a considerable 7 feet, and he could support huge weights. He temporarily relieved the giant **ATLAS** of carrying the heavens on his shoulders, and killed the giant **ANTAEUS** by hoisting him on his shoulders. He hence ornaments the Waag (Weigh House) in Amsterdam, and his figure was used to convey power and impenetrability at important entrances, and on arms and armour.

LEFT: **HERAKLES**'s exceptional strength was demonstrated in infancy when he crushed to death two serpents sent by a jealous **HERA** (Juno, visible through the window) to kill him and his twin brother Iphicles.

BELOW: Herakles and his twelve labours. After Hera made him kill his wife Megara and children, he visited the Oracle of Delphi, who told him to serve his cousin Eurytheus of Mycenae. 1. The Nemean Lion; 2. The Lernaean Hydra; 3. The Arcadian stag (Ceryneian Hind); 4. The Erymanthian Boar; 5. The Augean Stables; 6. The Stymphalian birds; 7. The Cretan bull; 8. The Mares of Diomedes; 9. The Girdle of Hippolyta; 10. Geryon's Cattle; 11. The Apples of the Hesperides; 12. Cerberus.

41

PAN – FAUNUS
god of all nature

The son of **HERMES** (*Mercury*) and the nymph **PENELOPEIA** (daughter of Dryopos "Oak-Face"), **PAN** (*Faunus*) was taken up to Olympus by Hermes (*Mercury, p.28*), where Dionysus (*Bacchus, p.36*) included him in his retinue. He was the lover of the goddess **SELENE** (*p.48*) and the nymph **ECHO** (who famously fell in love with Narcissus) amongst others (he had 'carnality with all creatures'). The principal rural divinity, allied to the Roman rustic deities *Faunus* and *Silvanus*, he ruled over Arcadia, an idyllic landscape inhabited by nymphs, fauns and shepherds.

Half man, half horny goat, Pan carries a crook and plays a seven-reed pipe—he was pursuing the chaste nymph **SYRINX** when naiads (river nymphs) saved her by transforming her into some hollow water reeds. Pan grabbed the reeds and turned them into his pipes.

A cheerful if louche and suggestive presence, Pan and his attributes frequently appear on garden ornaments. He is also often depicted with a phallus, and the figure was resuscitated by the pagan revival. When disturbed in lonely places like forests or wildernesses he can cause irrational terror (*panic*).

RIGHT: **PAN** *with a nymph holding a cornucopia, beside a term. His pipes, cymbals, and other possessions hang in the tree behind.*

EROS – CUPID
god of erotic love

EROS is the name of one of the primordial gods (*p.2*), and also the god of love, **EROS** (*Amor/Cupid*), son of **APHRODITE** (*Venus, p.20*) by **ARES** (*Mars, p.18*), and brother of **ANTEROS**, god of requited love. He loved and eventually married the superlatively beautiful Psyche (*see p.vi*).

Hesiod describes Eros as '*the most handsome among the immortal gods, dissolver of flesh, who overcomes the reason and purpose in the breasts of all gods and all men.*'

Often winged and sometimes blindfolded (love is blind) he rides a dolphin and shoots arrows from his golden bow or brings a burning torch. He is sometimes depicted as a mischievous child (*below left, with Aphrodite*), other times as a beautiful boy (*below right*). Piercing by his arrows causes consuming pangs of love, which not even **ZEUS** (*Jupiter*) can withstand. He kindles love between sexes, and also between men.

THE MUSES

goddesses of the arts and sciences

The nine MUSES preside over the Arts and Sciences, (humankind's civilizing aspects that make up a *Museum*). Daughters of ZEUS (*Jupiter, p.10*) and MNEMOSYNE (*Memory, below, with Zeus disguised as a shepherd*), the natural companions of Apollo, they inhabit Mount Parnassus.

CALLIOPE, the superior muse, represents epic poetry and science, and holds a roll of parchment and pen, as does CLIO, muse of history and storytelling, who broadcasts it with a trumpet; EUTERPE, muse of lyric poetry, holds an *aulos* (double flute); MELPOMENE, muse of tragedy, normally holds a tragic mask and club or sword, and plays a triangle; TERPISCHORE, muse of dance and chorus, and mother of the Sirens, has a lyre and plectrum; ERATO, muse of erotic poetry, geometry and mimic art, bears a large stringed instrument, or globes; THALIA, muse of comedy, most often has a comic mask, ivy garland and crook; POLYHYMNIA, muse of sacred poetry and sublime *hymn*, wears a closely wrapped dress and a serious expression and plays a viola da gamba; URANIA, muse of astronomy, holds a celestial globe and a small wand.

The Muses were a picturesque choice for the ornamentation of all things to do with culture.

44

URANIA   CLIO   EUTERPE

THALIA   MELPOMENE   TERPSICHORE

ERATO   POLYHYMNIA   CALLIOPE

45

JANUS
the two-faced god

One of the oldest Roman gods with no Greek equivalent, JANUS has two faces pointing opposite ways: one a youth (indicating beginnings), the other a bearded old man (for endings). He presides over all transitions, abstract, concrete, sacred and profane. January, the first month, is named for him; he was also invoked at daybreak, at the start of a season or when setting out on a voyage. Indeed, he can stand for time itself.

Since they mark transition, portals of all descriptions come under Janus's aegis. Often shown holding a key, he is the doorkeeper (*janitor*) and an appropriate addition to any entrance. A Janus head was also mounted on top of a term or boundary post to mark the beginning of a property. In ancient Rome there was a passageway dedicated to Janus, left open in times of war, so he could join the battle. When peace was concluded the gates were closed.

He is said to have married the nymph JUTURNA, whose healing spring was in the Roman Forum near the temple of Vesta. He also ravished the nymph CARDEA, against her will, but compensated her by giving her power over door hinges, together with a branch of flowering hawthorn to exclude evil from any threshold.

POMONA & VERTUMNUS
deities of fruitfulness

Two other Roman divinities with no Greek equivalents are to be found in the countryside. POMONA was the goddess of orchards and trees, protecting them and caring for their cultivation. She was particularly associated with the flourishing of fruit trees. Sometimes symbolising autumn, she also represents agriculture and fruitfulness.

She was married to VERTUMNUS, god of the seasons, of plant growth, blossom and the ripening of fruit. He had the power to shapeshift, and loved Pomona dearly, but she repeatedly rejected him. So after failing as a fruit picker, fisherman, farmer herdsman and vintner he finally succeeded after he metamorphosed into an old woman who counselled Pomona to reject all other suitors (including SILVANUS, *p.42*), and choose him, in the form of a beautiful young man.

FAR LEFT: **POMONA** and **VERTUMNUS**, Roman divinities of trees, seasonal growth and fruit.

LEFT: A Greek god who presided over the exuberant fertility of nature, gardens and vineyards, was large-phallused **PRIAPUS**, god of procreation, son of **DIONYSUS** and **APHRODITE**, protector of any in need. He could deflect the evil eye. He was similar to the marriage deity **MUTINUS**.

HELIOS, SELENE & EOS
sun, moon and dawn

Son of Titans **HYPERION** and **THEIA**, **HELIOS** (*Sol*) married **PERSE**, daughter of Oceanus and Tethys. Their children included **CIRCE** (the sorceress) and **PHAETON** (who crashed his father's chariot into the Earth, setting it ablaze, for which Zeus killed him with a thunderbolt).

Helios brings the light of day, rising in the East and crossing the heavens in a chariot drawn by four fiery horses before dipping down to his garden palace in the West, tended by the three nymphs of the setting sun, the **HESPERIDES: AEGLE**, **ERYTHEIA** and **HESPERIA**. A handsome youth, his head is crowned with rays and a cloak flies from his shoulders. The Colossus of Rhodes was a statue of Helios. From him we have *heliograph*, *heliotype*, *heliometer*, *heliocentric* and the flower *heliotrope*.

The moon goddess **SELENE** (*Luna*) was Helios' sister. She wears a crescent moon (or sometimes horns). Lover of both **PAN** (*p.42*) and **ZEUS** (*p.10*), she carries a torch as she nightly drives her chariot across the starry sky.

The third sibling was **EOS** (*Aurora*), bringer of dawn (*right*). Her floating cloth covered the moon and stars as she crossed the heavens. Consort of **ORION**, she bore the wind gods (*p.50*) by **ASTRAEUS**, god of the dusk (not to be confused with **ASTERIA**, Titan mother of Hecate, goddess of falling stars).

ABOVE: **HELIOS** (Sol) is often shown with his head crowned with twelve rays, representing the twelve signs of the zodiac through which he passes every year. Helios and Selene later became identified with **APOLLO** and **ARTEMIS**, who inherited some of their characteristics.

LEFT: **SELENE** (Luna). ABOVE: Altar showing Selene and Astraeus, flanked by the brothers, morning star **PHOSPHOROS** (Lucifer) and evening star **HESPEROS** (Vesper), sons of **EOS** (Aurora, top), apparitions of the planet Venus.

WIND GODS
north, south, east & west

The **ANEMOI** were the gods of the four cardinal winds (*see opposite*), the children of **EOS** (*Aurora, p.48*) and **ASTRAEUS**. Important divinities for seafarers, they were ruled over by **AEOLUS**, son of Poseidon (*lower, opposite*). **BOREAS** was the stormy winter north wind, ravisher of maidens, whereas **ZEPHYRUS** was the warm spring west wind. A winged head with puffed cheeks was shorthand for all winds

Zephyrus (*below left*) was marrried to the nymph **CHLORIS** (*Flora, below right*), daughter of Amphion and Niobe. He gifted her the power over all flowers—everything that blooms. She is ornamentally useful, often butterfly-winged, garlanded and holding a cornucopia of blossoms. She became significant as a goddess of fertility.

BOREAS (Aquilo) - the North Wind. God of Winter chills. Blows a conch shell.

EURUS (Vulturnus) - the unlucky East Wind. God of Autumn and hot storms.

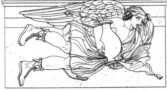

NOTUS (Auster) - the hot South Wind. God of Summer. With vase of summer rains.

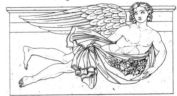

ZEPHYRUS (Favonius) - the West Wind. God of Spring breezes. Scatters flowers.

ABOVE: The cave of the winds on the island of Aeolia, home to **AEOLUS**, king of the winds. The hero **ODYSSEUS** (Ulysses) can be seen rowing his boat into the mouth of the cave. He obtained a bag of violent storm winds from Aeolus, but his companions later opened it, causing no end of trouble.

MOIRAI – PARCAE
destiny and fate

The three **MOIRAE** (*Parcae*), or Fates, were, according to Plato, the daughters of primordial **ANANKE** (*Fatum, p.3*), while other sources have their parents as **ZEUS** and **THEMIS**. Ananke was the personification of the unalterable force of destiny; a force meted out by the Moirae.

The three sisters are depicted together, holding the thread of life: birth, life itself and death. First is **CLOTHO** (*Nona*) the spinner, holding a distaff or spindle or alternatively, a scroll – the book of fate. Second is **LACHESIS** (*Decima*) who allots and measures out the length of life. Third is wrinkle-faced **ATROPOS** (*Morta*) who snips the thread with her teeth (*as below*) or with shears (*top right*). **Atropine** is the name given to the poisonous alkaloid found in deadly nightshade.

TYCHE – FORTUNA
goddess of fortune, chance and luck

Probably the daughter of ZEUS and APHRODITE, TYCHE (*Fortuna*) was the goddess of fortune, chance and luck. Her sisters were the MOIRAI (*Parcae, Fates, opposite*). She is often winged and blindfold (chance is random), and shown with a sphere or wheel (for instability). A *gubernaculum* (ship's rudder) illustrates her power to guide, a cornucopia indicates plenty. When adopted as the deity of a city, she wears a mural crown (like city walls). The revolving wheel of fortune shows how easily fortunes can change, the powerful can fall and the lowly rise. Her male equivalent was CAERUS (*Occasio*), the god of opportunity.

ABOVE: **PLUTUS**, *son of Demeter or Tyche, blind god of wealth. From him we have the words* **plutocrat**, **plutocracy** *and* **plutomania**.

THEMIS, DIKE & ASTRAEA
and Arete, Alethia, Eleutheria & Harmonia

The titan **THEMIS** (*Justitia*) was daughter of **URANUS** and **GAIA** and mother of the **HORAE** (*p.58*) and **MOIRAE** (*p.52*) by **ZEUS**. The earliest goddess of justice, law, custom and equity, she dwells on Olympus counselling Zeus, convening the gods and delivering oracles. Grave in expression, her attributes include the sword of justice and scales of impartiality. Her attributes were inherited by her Hora daughter **DIKE**, who was also shown blindfolded, a feature adopted for figures of Lady Justice from the 16th century, fronting law courts.

Dike was closely identified with the goddess **ASTREA** (*opposite*), who lived among mortals and became so horrified by their lawlessness that Zeus removed her to the constellation Virgo, as 'star-bright maiden'.

Many minor gods and goddesses who scarcely appeared in the myths, became personifications of subjects that fitted with their characteristics. Thus the goddess **ARETE** (*Virtus*) stood for moral excellence, **ALETHIA** (*Veritas*) for truth and reality, **ELEUTHERIA** (*Libertas*) for freedom, **HARMONIA** (*Concordia*) for harmony and concord. In the classical period these were useful on the reverse of coins (*below*), implying the standards of the ruler impressed on the obverse. Their skills and characteristics were illustrated by how they appeared. Arete was 'fair to see and of high bearing…sober was
her figure and her robe
was white'. Whereas her
counterpart **KAKIA** (*Cacia*,
Vice) was 'wearing purple
with painted cheeks'.

ABOVE: The Titan goddess **THEMIS**, goddess of custom and law. LEFT: **ASTRAEA** (Justitia), daughter of Eos (p. 48), goddess of justice. Both she and Themis are often shown with scales of impartiality and a sword of justice. Astraea's counterpart **DIKE** was also shown blindfolded.

LEFT: **ARETE** (Virtus), goddess of virtuous courage. As mother of the Virtues, Arete represents the highest ideals of the ethical life. Here she crushes deadly sins underfoot.

BELOW: **ALETHIA** (Veritas), goddess of truth, daughter of **CRONOS**, and mother of Arete.

ERINYES, NEMESIS & THANATOS
fury, revenge and death

The three avenging ERINYES (*Furiae* or *Dirae*) were born from the splashed blood of castrated CRONOS (*Uranus, p.8*). Brandishing whips and torches, with snakes writhing in their hair, they emerged from Erebus to mete out punishment to the living and the dead, ensuring their descent to Hades. They were euphemistically known as the EUMENIDES, 'the kindly ones', as they rid the world of evil-doers and protected the social order. TISIPHONE was avenger of murders, MEGAERA dealt with jealousy and envy, and ALEKTO unceasingly castigated crimes against the gods. Black sheep were sacrificed to them.

Children of Erebus and Nyx in the same line of were THANATOS (*Mors, opposite*), god of peaceful death, the KERES, female spirits who feasted on those who died violently, and NEMESIS (*Invidia, opposite*).

LEFT: **NEMESIS / ADRASTEIA** (Invidia), the goddess of retribution, sister of the Moirai. She carries a bridle, symbol of restraint. She visited with losses and suffering all who were blessed with too many gifts of fortune. Nemesis sometimes directed the Erinyes to do her bidding.

FACING PAGE: The **ERINYES** (Furies) approaching Tereus, who forced himself on his sister-in-law Philomena and cut out her tongue out to silence her.

BELOW: **HYPNOS** (Somnus, sleep) and his brother **THANATOS** (Mors, death) carry King Sarpedon, who was slain by Patroclus (companion of Achilles), while Hermes looks on. Thanatos was god of peaceful / noble death.

THE HORAE
the turning of the seasons

The daughters of Zeus and the Titan goddess of law, THEMIS *(p.54)*, the HORAE, "hours", usually appear as a group of three lithe, dancing, and garlanded maidens, representing the seasons. THALLO promoted the buds and shoots of Spring, AUXO the blooms of summer, and KARPO the fruitfulness of autumn. Winter, initially regarded as dormant, was later added as a fourth personification.

Three further names relate to the Horae. EUNOMIA stood for good order and lawful conduct; DIKE *(Justitia, p.54)* for justice and EIRENE *(Pax)*, the most cheerful of the Horae, for peace.

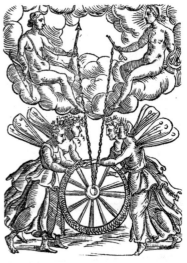

ABOVE: *The three ancient* HORAE, *or "hours", divine children of Zeus and Themis.* RIGHT: *The four later Horae, depicted as winged goddesses of the four seasons. They also presided over the revolution of the twelve hours and the twelve signs of the zodiac, represented here as a twelve-spoked wheel.*